Quiche Cookbook

A Savory Pie Cookbook Featuring Only Easy and Delicious Quiche Recipes

By
BookSumo Press

Published by
http://www.booksumo.com

LEGAL NOTES

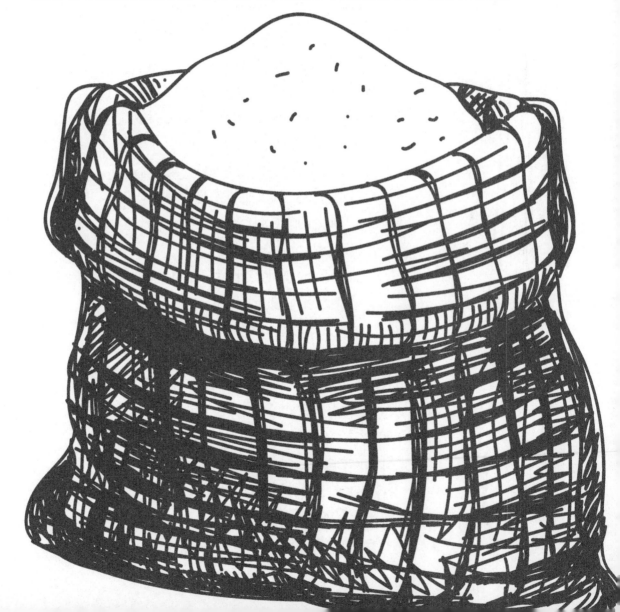

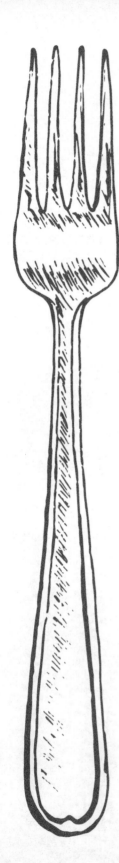

Table of Contents

The "Perfect" Quiche Crust 7
Autumn Acorn Quiche 8
Veggie Cheese Bites 9
Classical Baked Pear Dessert 10
Turkey Ham and Cheese Quiche I 11
Turkey Ham and Cheese Quiche II 12
A Quiche Of Mushrooms and Spinach 13
The Simplest Zucchini Quiche I 14
A Quiche of Chili's and Spinach 15
Crab Quiche I 16
A Quiche of Parmesan 17
A Quiche of Bacon and Swiss 18
Spinach Quiche 19
Crab Quiche II 20
A Classic Quiche 21
Zucchini Quiche 22
Seafood Quiche 23
A Quiche of Swiss and Ham 24
Zucchini Quiche II 25
Zucchini Pie 26
A Classic Quiche II 27
Ham and Cheese Quiche II 28
A Quiche of Bacon, Swiss, & Cheddar 29
Broccoli and Cheddar Quiche 30
Spinach Muenster Quiche 31
Spinach and Ham Quiche 32
Crab Quiche III 33
Vegetable Quiche Cups 34

Crab and Cheddar Quiche 35
Agrarian Quiche 36
Quiche a la Martinique 37
Mini Quiche II 38
A Quiche Without A Crust 39
Zucchini Quiche III 40
Quiche Quiche 41
Hash Brown Quiche 42
Nutmeg and Bacon Quiche 43
Cheddar Mushroom Quiche 44
Rustic Quiche 45
Seattle Style Quiche 46
Broccoli, Lentils, and Tomato Quiche 47
Pepper and Chicken Quiche 48
Creamy Romano and Swiss Quiche 49
Artisan Sun-Dried Pesto Quiche 50
A Quiche from Maine 51
Cherry Tomatoes and Kale Quiche 52
Nutty Honey Quiche 53
Nutty Tangy Chicken Quiche 54
Mexican Style Quiche 55
Artisan Style Spinach Quiche 56
Really Rustic Quiche 57
A Quiche of Squash and Mozzarella 58
Swiss and Bacon Quiche 59
Nova Scotia Quiche 60
Quiche I 61
A Quiche of Broccoli 62
Southern French Quiche 63
Southwest Quiches 64

Roasted Veggies Quiche 65
Algerian Quiche 66
Wonda's Award Winning Quiche 67
Lucia's Quiche Caprese 68
Monterey Mushroom Quiche 69
Marie's Quiche 70
Saint Claude Quiche 71
Los Angeles Monterey Quiche 72
Brown Ham Quiche 73
Pumpkin Quiche 74

The "Perfect" Quiche Crust

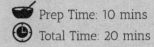

Prep Time: 10 mins
Total Time: 20 mins

Servings per Recipe: 6	
Calories	178 kcal
Carbohydrates	12 g
Cholesterol	35 mg
Fat	13.2 g
Protein	2.9 g
Sodium	111 mg

Ingredients

3/4 cup all-purpose flour
6 tbsps cold butter, cut into small pieces
1/4 cup shredded Cheddar cheese

5 tsps cold water

Directions

1. Preheat your oven at 350 degrees F and put some oil over the quiche dish.
2. Combine flour and butter in a bowl very thoroughly before adding grated cheese.
3. Add water spoon after spoon until you can form a ball out of it.
4. Wrap this dough with plastic wrap before refrigerating it for at least thirty minutes.
5. Roll this dough and put this in the quiche dish.
6. Bake in the preheated oven for about 10 minutes before filling it with quiche custard of your choice.

AUTUMN
Acorn Quiche

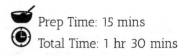

Prep Time: 15 mins
Total Time: 1 hr 30 mins

Servings per Recipe: 6

Calories	165 kcal
Carbohydrates	20 g
Cholesterol	142 mg
Fat	4.8 g
Protein	12.6 g
Sodium	69 mg

Ingredients

2 acorn squash
1 red onion, chopped
1 cup chopped cooked turkey
4 eggs

1 tbsp pumpkin pie spice
salt to taste

Directions

1. Preheat your oven at 350 degrees F and put some oil over the quiche dish.

2. Put squash into a baking dish and then bake it in the preheated oven for one full hour before cutting this in half, removing seeds and scrapping the meat out in a bowl.

3. Combine squash, turkey, eggs, pumpkin pie spice, onion and salt together in a medium sized bowl before pouring this mixture into the quiche dish

4. Bake in the preheated oven for about 45 minutes or until the top of the quiche is golden brown in color.

Veggie Cheese Bites

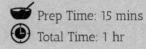

Prep Time: 15 mins
Total Time: 1 hr

Servings per Recipe: 6
Calories	530 kcal
Carbohydrates	23.8 g
Cholesterol	196 mg
Fat	36.5 g
Protein	28.2 g
Sodium	1068 mg

Ingredients

1/4 cup butter
2 (10 ounce) packages frozen broccoli florets, thawed and drained
1 pound shredded sharp Cheddar cheese
1 cup milk
1 cup all-purpose flour

3 eggs
1 tsp baking powder
1 tsp salt
ground black pepper to taste

Directions

1. Preheat your oven at 350 degrees F and put some oil over the quiche dish.
2. Combine broccoli, milk, flour, eggs, baking powder, salt, Cheddar cheese and black pepper in medium sized bowl.
3. Pour this mixture in the quiche dish over melted butter.
4. Bake in the preheated oven for about 45 minutes or until the top of the quiche is golden brown in color.
5. Serve.

CLASSICAL
Baked Pear Dessert

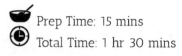
Prep Time: 15 mins
Total Time: 1 hr 30 mins

Servings per Recipe: 4
Calories   206 kcal
Carbohydrates   34.5 g
Cholesterol   23 mg
Fat   8.9 g
Protein   0.8 g
Sodium   64 mg

Ingredients

4 Bosc pears
2 tbsps honey
3 tbsps butter, melted
dash ground ginger

Directions

1. Preheat your oven at 375 degrees F and put some oil over the quiche dish.
2. Peel and cut a portion off of the bottom of your pears so that they can stand straight, and place them in the baking dish.
3. Pour melted butter, honey and some ground ginger over these pears before covering the dish with aluminum foil.
4. Bake in the preheated oven for about one hour or until the top is golden brown in color.

Turkey Ham and Cheese Quiche I

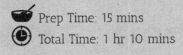 Prep Time: 15 mins

Total Time: 1 hr 10 mins

Servings per Recipe: 10	
Calories	286 kcal
Carbohydrates	15.6 g
Cholesterol	110 mg
Fat	25.2 g
Protein	11 g
Sodium	422 mg

Ingredients

2 (12 ounce) packages frozen country style shredded hash brown potatoes

1/3 cup butter, melted

1/2 cup heavy whipping cream

2 eggs

1 cup diced cooked ham

1 cup shredded Monterey Jack and Cheddar cheese blend

Directions

1. Preheat your oven at 425 degrees F and put some oil over the quiche dish.
2. Put a mixture of potatoes and butter in the quiche dish as a crust.
3. Bake this in the preheated oven for about 25 minutes.
4. Combine cream and eggs in a bowl before mixing it with the potatoes in a bowl.
5. Form a layer of ham and Monterey Jack cheese in the quiche dish before pouring this mixture over it.
6. Bake in the preheated oven for about 30 minutes or until the top of the quiche is golden brown in color.

TURKEY HAM
and Cheese Quiche II (Low Cholesterol)

Prep Time: 15 mins
Total Time: 1 hr 20 mins

Servings per Recipe: 8

Calories	261 kcal
Carbohydrates	14.3 g
Cholesterol	20 mg
Fat	16.3 g
Protein	13.7 g
Sodium	602 mg

Ingredients

1 prepared 9-inch single pie crust
1 tbsp olive oil
4 green onions, chopped
1/2 pound cooked turkey ham, cubed
1 cup fat-free egg substitute
7 fluid ounces fat-free evaporated milk

1/4 cup shredded part-skim mozzarella cheese
1 tbsp grated Parmesan cheese
1 tsp chopped fresh chives (optional)

Directions

1. Preheat your oven at 325 degrees F and put some oil over the quiche dish before pressing pie crust into it.
2. Cook green onions in hot oil for about 3 minutes before adding this on top of ham that is spread on the pie crust.
3. Pour a mixture of mozzarella cheese, egg substitute and evaporated milk over the ham mixture before adding Parmesan cheese and chives.
4. Bake in the preheated oven for about 20 minutes before turning the heat up to 350 Degrees F and baking for another 20 minutes or until the top of the quiche is golden brown in color.
5. Allow it to set for thirty minutes before serving.

A Quiche Of Mushrooms and Spinach

Prep Time: 15 mins
Total Time: 50 mins

Servings per Recipe: 9
Calories	325 kcal
Carbohydrates	10.8 g
Cholesterol	139 mg
Fat	22.5 g
Protein	20.9 g
Sodium	806 mg

Ingredients

6 slices bacon
4 eggs, beaten
1 1/2 cups light cream
1/4 tsp ground nutmeg
1/2 tsp salt
1/2 tsp pepper
2 cups chopped fresh spinach

2 cups chopped fresh mushrooms
1/2 cup chopped onions
1 cup shredded Swiss cheese
1 cup shredded Cheddar cheese
1 (9 inch) deep dish pie crust

Directions

1. Preheat your oven at 400 degrees F and put some oil over the quiche dish.
2. Cook bacon over medium heat until brown and then crumble it after draining.
3. Mix eggs, pepper, cream, salt, nutmeg, bacon, spinach, mushrooms, 3/4 cup Swiss cheese, 3/4 cup Cheddar cheese and onions in a bowl very thoroughly.
4. Pour this mixture over the pie crust and add some cheese.
5. Bake in the preheated oven for about 35 minutes or until the top of the quiche is golden brown in color.

THE SIMPLEST
Zucchini Quiche I

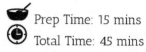

Prep Time: 15 mins
Total Time: 45 mins

Servings per Recipe: 9
Calories	314 kcal
Carbohydrates	15.7 g
Cholesterol	188 mg
Fat	22 g
Protein	13.6 g
Sodium	364 mg

Ingredients

2 cups grated zucchini
1 (9 inch) pie shell, unbaked
6 eggs, beaten

1 cup shredded Cheddar cheese

Directions

1. Preheat your oven at 350 degrees F and put some oil over the quiche dish.
2. Put zucchini evenly in quiche dish before adding eggs and some cheddar cheese.
3. Bake in the preheated oven for about 30 minutes or until the top of the quiche is golden brown in color.

A Quiche
of Chili's and
Spinach

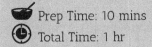 Prep Time: 10 mins

Total Time: 1 hr

Servings per Recipe: 18	
Calories	324 kcal
Carbohydrates	16.3 g
Cholesterol	173 mg
Fat	22.9 g
Protein	14 g
Sodium	786 mg

Ingredients

1/2 cup all-purpose flour
1 tsp baking powder
1 tsp salt
12 eggs
1 (8 ounce) package shredded Colby-Monterey Jack cheese
2 cups small curd cottage cheese

1 (10 ounce) package frozen chopped spinach, thawed and drained
2 (4 ounce) cans chopped green chilies
1/2 cup melted butter
2 (9 inch) unbaked pie crusts

Directions

1. Preheat your oven at 400 degrees F and put some oil over the quiche dish before setting aside a mixture of salt, flour and baking powder.
2. Whisk eggs and flour mixture together thoroughly before adding Colby-Monterey Jack cheese, spinach, green chills, cottage cheese and melted butter into it.
3. Pour this mixture evenly into the quiche dishes.
4. Bake in the preheated oven for about 15 minutes before turning the heat down to 350 Degrees F and baking for another 40 minutes or until the top of the quiche is golden brown in color.

CRAB
Quiche I

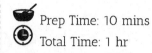 Prep Time: 10 mins

Total Time: 1 hr

Servings per Recipe: 6

Calories	326 kcal
Carbohydrates	14.3 g
Cholesterol	83 mg
Fat	24.8 g
Protein	11.8 g
Sodium	308 mg

Ingredients

1/2 cup mayonnaise
2 tbsps all-purpose flour
2 eggs, beaten
1/2 cup milk
1 cup crab meat
1 cup diced Swiss cheese

1/2 cup chopped green onions
1 (9 inch) unbaked pie crust

Directions

1. Preheat your oven at 350 degrees F and put some oil over the quiche dish.
2. Whisk eggs, milk, mayonnaise, crab, flour, onion and cheese very thoroughly.
3. Pour this mixture in the quiche dish.
4. Bake in the preheated oven for about 30 minutes or until the top of the quiche is golden brown in color.

A Quiche of Parmesan

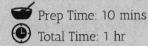
Prep Time: 10 mins
Total Time: 1 hr

Servings per Recipe: 6

Calories	371 kcal
Carbohydrates	12.5 g
Cholesterol	161 mg
Fat	26.6 g
Protein	21 g
Sodium	797 mg

Ingredients

2 cups milk
4 eggs
3/4 cup biscuit baking mix
1/4 cup butter, softened
1 cup grated Parmesan cheese
1 (10 ounce) package chopped frozen broccoli, thawed and drained

1 cup cubed cooked ham
8 ounces shredded Cheddar cheese

Directions

1. Preheat your oven to 375 degrees F and put some oil over the quiche dish.
2. Now mix milk, eggs, parmesan cheese, baking mix and some butter in a bowl and then add broccoli, cheddar cheese and ham.
3. Mix thoroughly and bake in the preheated oven for about 50 minutes or until the top of the quiche is golden brown in color.

A QUICHE
of Bacon and Swiss

 Prep Time: 15 mins
Total Time: 50 mins

Servings per Recipe: 6
Calories	291 kcal
Carbohydrates	12.9 g
Cholesterol	170 mg
Fat	18.8 g
Protein	17 g
Sodium	804 mg

Ingredients

8 slices bacon
4 ounces shredded Swiss cheese
2 tbsps butter, melted
4 eggs, beaten
1/4 cup finely chopped onion
1 tsp salt

1/2 cup all-purpose flour
1 1/2 cups milk

Directions

1. Preheat your oven to 375 degrees F and put some oil over the quiche dish.
2. Cook bacon over medium heat until brown and then crumble.
3. Put cheese and this crumbled bacon at the bottom of the dish and now mix milk, eggs, onion, salt and some butter in a bowl and add into the pan.
4. Bake in the preheated oven for about 35 minutes or until the top of the quiche is golden brown in color.

Spinach
Quiche

Prep Time: 10 mins
Total Time: 1 hr 10 mins

Servings per Recipe: 8	
Calories	231 kcal
Carbohydrates	6.1 g
Cholesterol	131 mg
Fat	14.9 g
Protein	19.1 g
Sodium	478 mg

Ingredients

1 (10 ounce) package frozen chopped spinach, thawed
1 bunch green onions, finely chopped (white parts only)
4 eggs, beaten

1 (16 ounce) package cottage cheese
2 cups shredded Cheddar cheese
1/4 cup crushed croutons

Directions

1. Preheat your oven to 375 degrees F and put some oil over the quiche dish.
2. Cook spinach over medium heat until soft and now mix cheddar cheese, eggs, onion, salt and some cottage cheese in a bowl and pour this into the pan
3. Mix it thoroughly and bake in the preheated oven for about one hour or until the top of the quiche is golden brown in color.

CRAB
Quiche II

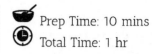 Prep Time: 10 mins

Total Time: 1 hr

Servings per Recipe: 6
Calories	346 kcal
Carbohydrates	16.9 g
Cholesterol	154 mg
Fat	26.1 g
Protein	11.4 g
Sodium	691 mg

Ingredients

1 (9 inch pie) deep dish frozen pie crust
4 eggs
1 cup heavy cream
1/2 tsp salt
1/2 tsp black pepper
3 dashes hot pepper sauce (e.g. Tabasco™), or to taste

1 cup shredded Monterey Jack cheese
1/4 cup grated Parmesan cheese
1 (8 ounce) package imitation crabmeat, flaked
1 green onion, chopped

Directions

1. Preheat your oven to 375 degrees F and put some oil over the quiche dish.
2. Bake pie crust for about 10 minutes to get it crispy
3. Now mix shredded cheese, eggs, onion, salt, cream, pepper, imitation crab and hot sauce in a bowl and pour this into baked pie.
4. Bake in the preheated oven for about 30 minutes or until the top of the quiche is golden brown in color and an additional 30 minutes in the oven after turning it off.

A Classic
Quiche

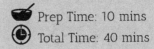 Prep Time: 10 mins
Total Time: 40 mins

Servings per Recipe: 8
Calories	212 kcal
Carbohydrates	12.7 g
Cholesterol	91 mg
Fat	15.7 g
Protein	5.4 g
Sodium	211 mg

Ingredients

1 tbsp butter
1 large onion, diced
3 eggs
1/3 cup heavy cream

1/3 cup shredded Swiss cheese
1 (9 inch pie) unbaked pie crust

Directions

1. Preheat your oven to 375 degrees F and put some oil over the quiche dish.
2. Melt butter over medium heat and then cook onions in it until soft.
3. Now whisk eggs and cream together in a bowl and then add cheese.
4. Place onion at the bottom of the dish and pour this mixture over it.
5. Bake in the preheated oven for about 30 minutes or until the top of the quiche is golden brown in color.

ZUCCHINI
Quiche

Prep Time: 10 mins
Total Time: 45 mins

Servings per Recipe: 6
Calories	272 kcal
Carbohydrates	15.4 g
Cholesterol	129 mg
Fat	20.1 g
Protein	8.4 g
Sodium	635 mg

Ingredients

1 cup biscuit baking mix
1 tsp dried oregano
1 tsp seasoning salt
1/2 tsp garlic powder
1/4 tsp salt
1 tsp dried parsley
1/3 cup grated Parmesan cheese

1/2 cup grated onion
4 eggs, beaten
1/3 cup vegetable oil
1 zucchini, sliced into rounds

Directions

1. Preheat your oven to 375 degrees F and put some oil over the quiche dish.
2. Combine biscuit mix, seasoning salt, garlic powder, salt, oregano, parsley, Parmesan cheese, eggs and onion in a bowl.
3. Now add zucchini and put this in the dish.
4. Bake in the preheated oven for about 30 minutes or until the top of the quiche is golden brown in color.

Seafood Quiche

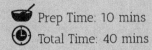 Prep Time: 10 mins

Total Time: 40 mins

Servings per Recipe: 6

Calories	95 kcal
Carbohydrates	8.2 g
Cholesterol	80 mg
Fat	2.8 g
Protein	8.9 g
Sodium	183 mg

Ingredients

6 ounces crabmeat
1/2 cup bread crumbs
1/2 cup milk
2 eggs, beaten
2 tbsps chopped fresh parsley
1 tbsp lemon juice
1 tsp prepared mustard

1/4 tsp Worcestershire sauce
salt to taste
ground black pepper to taste
1 pinch pie cayenne pepper
1 pinch pie paprika

Directions

1. Preheat your oven to 400 degrees F and put some oil over the quiche dish.
2. Remove any shells or cartilage that you may find from the crab meat.
3. Combine all the ingredients except paprika which are mentioned; in a bowl and pour this mixture into the prepared dish.
4. Bake in the preheated oven for about 30 minutes or until the top of the quiche is golden brown in color.

A QUICHE
of Swiss and Ham

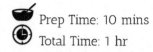

Prep Time: 10 mins
Total Time: 1 hr

Servings per Recipe: 4
Calories	611 kcal
Carbohydrates	33.4 g
Cholesterol	189 mg
Fat	41.8 g
Protein	25.3 g
Sodium	663 mg

Ingredients

1 sheet frozen puff pastry, thawed
1 cup milk
3 eggs
1/4 cup frozen chopped spinach,
thawed and drained
salt and ground black pepper to taste
1 cup shredded Swiss cheese

3/4 cup chopped cooked ham
1 small tomato, sliced (optional)

Directions

1. Preheat your oven to 400 degrees F and put some oil over the quiche dish after putting some puff pastry at the bottom of the baking dish.
2. Combine milk, salt, eggs and spinach in a bowl very thoroughly and pour this mixture over the puff after adding a cheese and ham layer.
3. Bake in the preheated oven for about 30 minutes or until the top of the quiche is golden brown in color.

Zucchini
Quiche II

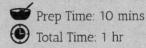 Prep Time: 10 mins
Total Time: 1 hr

Servings per Recipe: 6
Calories	314 kcal
Carbohydrates	15.7 g
Cholesterol	188 mg
Fat	22 g
Protein	13.6 g
Sodium	364 mg

Ingredients

2 cups grated zucchini
1 (9 inch pie) pie shell, unbaked
6 eggs, beaten

1 cup shredded Cheddar cheese

Directions

1. Preheat your oven to 400 degrees F and put some oil over the quiche dish.
2. Put some zucchini at bottom of the dish and add eggs and some cheddar cheese over it.
3. Bake in the preheated oven for about 30 minutes or until the top of the quiche is golden brown in color.

ZUCCHINI
Pie

 Prep Time: 10 mins
Total Time: 1 hr 10 mins

Servings per Recipe: 8
Calories	410 kcal
Carbohydrates	16.2 g
Cholesterol	157 mg
Fat	31.5 g
Protein	16.6 g
Sodium	902 mg

Ingredients

1 (10 inch pie) unbaked pie crust
2 tbsps butter, melted
2/3 cup bacon bits
4 cups diced zucchini
4 eggs
1/2 cup heavy cream
1/2 tsp dried marjoram

1 tsp onion salt
1/4 tsp cayenne pepper
2 cups shredded Cheddar cheese

Directions

1. Preheat your oven to 400 degrees F and put some oil over the quiche dish.
2. Put some crumbled bacon in the dish and then blend cream, zucchini and eggs very thoroughly.
3. Now add marjoram, cayenne, onion salt and this mix together.
4. Also add some cheese and pour this into the dish.
5. Bake in the preheated oven for about 30 minutes or until the top of the quiche is golden brown in color.

A Classic
Quiche II

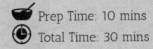 Prep Time: 10 mins
Total Time: 30 mins

Servings per Recipe: 12
Calories   123 kcal
Carbohydrates   15 g
Cholesterol   68 mg
Fat   4.2 g
Protein   6.1 g
Sodium   233 mg

Ingredients

12 slices bread
1 onion, grated
1/2 cup shredded Swiss cheese
1 cup milk

4 eggs
1 tsp dry mustard
1 pinch pie black pepper

Directions

1. Preheat your oven to 400 degrees F and put some oil over the muffin tins.
2. Now cut some circles from the bread and put these circles into these muffins tin.
3. Put shredded cheese and onion evenly in all the tins.
4. Now add a mixture of milk, pepper, eggs and mustard into all the tins evenly.
5. Bake in the preheated oven for about 30 minutes or until the top of the quiche is golden brown in color.

HAM
and Cheese
Quiche II

Prep Time: 15 mins
Total Time: 1 hr 10 mins

Servings per Recipe: 6
Calories	283 kcal
Carbohydrates	14.3 g
Cholesterol	103 mg
Fat	20.1 g
Protein	11.3 g
Sodium	621 mg

Ingredients

2 tbsps all-purpose flour
1/2 tsp salt
1 cup half-and-half
3 eggs
2 slices Swiss cheese
1 recipe pastry for a 9 inch pie single
crust pie

1/2 cup chopped fresh spinach
1/2 cup canned mushrooms
1 (4.5 ounce) can ham, flaked
1/2 cup shredded Cheddar cheese

Directions

1. Preheat your oven to 350 degrees F and put some oil over the quiche dish.
2. Combine flour, eggs, salt and half-and-half in a bowl of medium size
3. Put spinach over Swiss cheese in the baking dish and then add mushrooms.
4. Pour the previous mixture into it and add flaked ham and some cheddar cheese over it
5. Bake in the preheated oven for about 55 minutes or until the top of the quiche is golden brown in color.

A Quiche
of Bacon, Swiss, & Cheddar

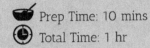 Prep Time: 10 mins

Total Time: 1 hr

Servings per Recipe: 6
Calories	462 kcal
Carbohydrates	20.2 g
Cholesterol	183 mg
Fat	31.5 g
Protein	24.7 g
Sodium	993 mg

Ingredients

1 (3 ounce) can bacon bits
1/2 cup chopped onion
5 ounces shredded Swiss cheese
3 ounces grated Cheddar cheese
1 (9 inch pie) deep dish frozen pie crust

4 eggs, lightly beaten
1 cup half-and-half cream

Directions

1. Preheat your oven to 400 degrees F and put some oil over the quiche dish.
2. Pour mixture of eggs and half-and-half over the mixture of both cheeses, bacon and onion in the dish.
3. Bake in the preheated oven for about 15 minutes and then an additional 35 minutes at 350 degrees F or until the top of the quiche is golden brown in color.

BROCCOLI
and Cheddar
Quiche

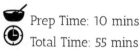 Prep Time: 10 mins

Total Time: 55 mins

Servings per Recipe: 8

Calories	401 kcal
Carbohydrates	10.6 g
Cholesterol	202 mg
Fat	32.4 g
Protein	19.3 g
Sodium	796 mg

Ingredients

1 cup sliced fresh mushrooms
1 cup chopped onions
1 cup chopped broccoli
5 eggs
1/3 cup MIRACLE WHIP Calorie-Wise
Dressing
1/3 cup milk

1 cup KRAFT Double Cheddar Shredded
Cheese Light
1 frozen deep-dish pie crust (9 inch pie)

Directions

1. Preheat your oven to 400 degrees F and put some oil over the quiche dish.
2. Cook all the vegetables in hot oil over medium heat for about 5 minutes.
3. Now add this mixture of vegetables and cheese into the mixture of eggs, milk and dressing.
4. Put this into the baking dish
5. Bake in the preheated oven for about 45 minutes or until the top of the quiche is golden brown in color.

Spinach Muenster Quiche

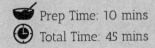 Prep Time: 10 mins
Total Time: 45 mins

Servings per Recipe: 8
Calories	311 kcal
Carbohydrates	4.5 g
Cholesterol	122 mg
Fat	25.4 g
Protein	17.8 g
Sodium	484 mg

Ingredients

8 ounces Muenster cheese, sliced
2 (10 ounce) packages frozen chopped spinach, thawed and drained
2 eggs
1/3 cup grated Parmesan cheese
1 (8 ounce) package cream cheese, softened
salt and pepper to taste
garlic powder to taste
4 ounces Muenster cheese, sliced

Directions

1. Preheat your oven to 350 degrees F and put some oil over the quiche dish.
2. Put Muenster cheese slices into the dish and then pour into it the mixture of spinach (all water drained), eggs, Parmesan cheese, cream cheese, salt, pepper and garlic powder.
3. Bake in the preheated oven for about 30 minutes or until the top of the quiche is golden brown in color.

SPINACH
and Ham Quiche

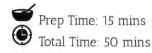 Prep Time: 15 mins
Total Time: 50 mins

Servings per Recipe: 6
Calories	275 kcal
Carbohydrates	15.7 g
Cholesterol	129 mg
Fat	16.4 g
Protein	16.9 g
Sodium	682 mg

Ingredients

1 (10 ounce) package frozen chopped spinach, thawed and drained
1 1/2 cups milk
1 cup diced cooked ham
3 eggs, beaten
3/4 cup baking mix (such as Bisquick ®)

1/2 cup chopped onion
1/2 cup shredded sharp Cheddar cheese
1/2 cup shredded Monterey Jack cheese

Directions

1. Preheat your oven to 350 degrees F and put some oil over the quiche dish.
2. Make a layer of spinach over the dish and then pour mixture of milk, ham, baking mix, onion, eggs, Cheddar cheese, and Monterey Jack over this layer.
3. Bake in the preheated oven for about 30 minutes or until the top of the quiche is golden brown in color.

Crab Quiche III

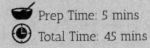 Prep Time: 5 mins

Total Time: 45 mins

Servings per Recipe: 8
Calories	396 kcal
Carbohydrates	20.9 g
Cholesterol	88 mg
Fat	29.4 g
Protein	12.4 g
Sodium	602 mg

Ingredients

1 (9 inch pie) deep dish pie crust
2 eggs, beaten
1/2 cup milk
1/2 cup mayonnaise
1 tsp cornstarch

1 1/2 cups shredded Swiss cheese
1/2 pound imitation crabmeat
1 pinch pie ground black pepper

Directions

1. Preheat your oven to 350 degrees F and put some oil over the quiche dish.
2. Mix eggs, cornstarch, cheese, pepper, mayonnaise, milk and imitation crabmeat thoroughly.
3. Pour this mixture into the baking dish.
4. Bake in the preheated oven for about 30 minutes or until the top of the quiche is golden brown in color.

VEGETABLE
Quiche Cups

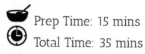

Prep Time: 15 mins
Total Time: 35 mins

Servings per Recipe: 6
Calories	69 kcal
Carbohydrates	3.4 g
Cholesterol	3 mg
Fat	2.4 g
Protein	9.1 g
Sodium	189 mg

Ingredients

cooking spray
1 (10 ounce) package frozen chopped
spinach, thawed and drained
3/4 cup liquid egg substitute
3/4 cup shredded reduced-fat Cheddar
cheese
1/4 cup diced onion

1/4 cup chopped green bell pepper
3 drops hot pepper sauce(optional)

Directions

1. Preheat your oven to 350 degrees F and put some oil over the muffin tins.
2. Combine all the ingredients mentioned above in a bowl and then divide it evenly among all the muffin tins.
3. Bake in the preheated oven for about 20 minutes or until the top of the quiche is golden brown in color.

Crab
and Cheddar Quiche

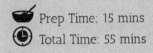 Prep Time: 15 mins

Total Time: 55 mins

Servings per Recipe: 8

Calories	333 kcal
Carbohydrates	13.7 g
Cholesterol	104 mg
Fat	25.7 g
Protein	12 g
Sodium	453 mg

Ingredients

1 (9 inch pie) unbaked pie crust
3 eggs
1/2 cup mayonnaise
1/2 cup whole milk
2 tbsps all-purpose flour
1 tsp seafood seasoning (such as Old Bay®)

1 cup shredded Cheddar cheese
1/2 cup chopped fresh parsley
1 cup crabmeat
1 pinch pie seafood seasoning (such as Old Bay®), or to taste

Directions

1. Preheat your oven to 350 degrees F and put some oil over the quiche dish.
2. Whisk eggs, 1 tsp seafood seasoning, milk and flour thoroughly and then add some cheddar cheese and parsley.
3. Fold crab meat in this mixture and pour it over the prepared dish, and also add some seafood seasoning over it.
4. Bake in the preheated oven for about 45 minutes or until the top of the quiche is golden brown in color.

AGRARIAN
Quiche

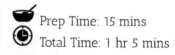 Prep Time: 15 mins

Total Time: 1 hr 5 mins

Servings per Recipe: 6

Calories	506 kcal
Carbohydrates	29.7 g
Cholesterol	134 mg
Fat	34.1 g
Protein	20.6 g
Sodium	627 mg

Ingredients

1 tbsp butter
1 large sweet onion (such as Vidalia®),
cut into chunks
6 eggs
1/2 cup whole milk
10 ounces shredded Jarlsberg cheese
2 ounces freshly grated Parmesan
cheese
2 bunches Swiss chard, stems and
leaves separated

1 tsp fresh thyme leaves
1 pinch pie nutmeg
salt and ground black pepper to taste
1 prepared 10-inch pie pie crust

Directions

1. Preheat your oven to 375 degrees F and put some oil over the quiche dish.
2. Cook onion in hot butter over medium heat for about 7 minutes and then place it in a large sized bowl
3. Blend parmesan cheese, eggs, milk and jarlsberg cheese in a blender until required smoothness is achieved and then add this into the bowl containing onion.
4. Now add black pepper, nutmeg, salt and some thyme into it and mix it thoroughly before pouring this mixture into the baking dish.
5. Bake in the preheated oven for about 45 minutes or until the top of the quiche is golden brown in color.

Quiche
a la Martinique

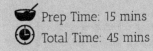 Prep Time: 15 mins

Total Time: 45 mins

Servings per Recipe: 6
Calories   239 kcal
Carbohydrates   18.8 g
Cholesterol   111 mg
Fat   14.9 g
Protein   7.8 g
Sodium   287 mg

Ingredients

1 (9 inch pie) unbaked 9 inch pie pie crust
1/2 cup shredded Swiss cheese
1/2 onion, minced
1 (4.5 ounce) can sliced mushrooms, drained
3 egg yolks
2 egg whites

2 tbsps all-purpose flour
2 tbsps milk
1/2 tsp chopped fresh thyme
salt and pepper to taste

Directions

1. Preheat your oven to 350 degrees F and put some oil over the quiche dish.
2. Make a layer of cheese, mushrooms and onions in the baking dish and pour mixture of eggs whites, milk, yolks and flour over it.
3. Spread it evenly and then add thyme, pepper and some salt.
4. Bake in the preheated oven for about 30 minutes or until the top of the quiche is golden brown in color.

MINI
Quiche II

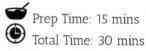
Servings per Recipe: 8
Calories	401 kcal
Carbohydrates	10.6 g
Cholesterol	202 mg
Fat	32.4 g
Protein	19.3 g
Sodium	796 mg

Ingredients

15 mini phyllo tart shells
1/2 cup shredded Swiss cheese
1/3 cup crumbled cooked bacon
1 egg
1/2 cup half-and-half
1/4 tsp dried basil
1/4 tsp dried parsley

1/4 tsp garlic powder
1/4 tsp salt
1/8 tsp ground black pepper

Directions

1. Preheat your oven to 350 degrees F and put some oil over the quiche dish.
2. Put phyllo tart shells in the baking dish and in each shell put one tsp of Swiss cheese and half a tsp of bacon
3. Whisk egg, half-and-half, basil, parsley, garlic powder, salt, and black pepper lightly in a bowl and put tsp of this mixture in each shell.
4. Add contents to your baking dish.
5. Bake in the preheated oven for about 15 minutes or until the top of the quiche is lightly brown in color.

A Quiche
Without A Crust

🥣 Prep Time: 15 mins
🕐 Total Time: 1 hr 15 mins

Servings per Recipe: 6
Calories   401 kcal
Carbohydrates   10.6 g
Cholesterol   202 mg
Fat   32.4 g
Protein   19.3 g
Sodium   796 mg

Ingredients

4 eggs
1 (16 ounce) container sour cream
1 (10 ounce) package frozen chopped spinach, thawed and drained
1 cup shredded Cheddar cheese
1/2 cup crumbled feta cheese
1/2 cup shredded Parmesan cheese
1/2 cup chopped onion
1/2 cup chopped tomato

1 (4 ounce) can canned chopped green chiles, drained
1 tsp minced garlic
1 tsp ground cumin
1 tbsp paprika
1/4 tsp cayenne pepper

Directions

1. Preheat your oven to 325 degrees F and put some oil over the quiche dish.
2. Whisk eggs and sour cream in a bowl until smooth and then add all the remaining ingredients into this bowl.
3. Mix everything thoroughly and then place contents into your baking dish.
4. Bake in the preheated oven for about 1 hour or until the top of the quiche is golden brown in color.

ZUCCHINI
Quiche III

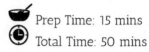

Prep Time: 15 mins
Total Time: 50 mins

Servings per Recipe: 8
Calories	272 kcal
Carbohydrates	14 g
Cholesterol	107 mg
Fat	19.1 g
Protein	12.2 g
Sodium	426 mg

Ingredients

6 cups grated zucchini
2 cups shredded Swiss cheese
4 eggs, beaten
1 cup biscuit baking mix (such as Bisquick®)

1/4 cup canola oil
1/2 tsp salt
1/4 tsp Italian seasoning

Directions

1. Preheat your oven to 350 degrees F and put some oil over the quiche dish.
2. Combine all the ingredients mentioned above thoroughly and then pour into the baking dish.
3. Bake in the preheated oven for about 35 minutes or until the top of the quiche is golden brown in color.

Quiche
Quiche

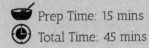
Prep Time: 15 mins
Total Time: 45 mins

Servings per Recipe: 9

Calories	401 kcal
Carbohydrates	18.8 g
Cholesterol	177 mg
Fat	29.3 g
Protein	15.8 g
Sodium	379 mg

Ingredients

4 eggs
2 cups half-and-half cream
1/8 tsp salt
1/4 tsp white pepper
1/8 tsp ground nutmeg

4 ounces Jarlsberg cheese, shredded
2 ounces mozzarella cheese, shredded
1 (9 inch pie) unbaked pie shell

Directions

1. Preheat your oven to 425 degrees F and put some oil over the quiche dish.
2. Whisk eggs and half-and-half until smooth in a bowl; add salt, nutmeg, and white pepper into it.
3. Place shredded Jarlsberg and mozzarella in the bowl, and mix evenly before adding contents to your baking dish.
4. Bake in the preheated oven for about 15 minutes and then cook for another 25 minutes at 350 degrees F or until the top of the quiche is golden brown in color.

HASH BROWN
Quiche

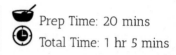

Prep Time: 20 mins
Total Time: 1 hr 5 mins

Servings per Recipe: 4

Calories	525 kcal
Fat	42.5 g
Carbohydrates	23.3g
Protein	27.9 g
Cholesterol	320 mg
Sodium	1722 mg

Ingredients

1 (16 oz.) package frozen shredded hash brown potatoes, thawed
1/4 C. butter, melted
5 eggs, lightly beaten
1 1/2 C. shredded Swiss cheese

1 C. cooked ham
1/4 C. milk
salt and pepper to taste

Directions

1. Coat a pie dish with oil and then set your oven to 375 degrees before doing anything else.
2. Fill your pie dish with the potatoes and press them down to form a crust.
3. Now coat the potatoes with melted butter.
4. Cook the pie dish in the oven for 17 mins.
5. Now get a bowl, combine: pepper, whisked eggs, salt, milk, ham, and cheese.
6. Enter this mix into the pie dish, over the potatoes, and cook the quiche in the oven for 22 more mins.
7. Enjoy.

Nutmeg
and Bacon Quiche

Prep Time: 15 mins
Total Time: 1 hr 40 mins

Servings per Recipe: 8

Calories	545 kcal
Fat	36.8 g
Carbohydrates	21.2g
Protein	31.2 g
Cholesterol	160 mg
Sodium	1023 mg

Ingredients

1 (9 in.) frozen pie crust, thawed
1 3/4 lbs sliced bacon
3 eggs, lightly beaten
1 (12 oz.) can evaporated milk
1/2 tsp spicy brown mustard

1/4 tsp ground nutmeg
1/2 C. all-purpose flour, or as needed
1 1/2 C. shredded Swiss cheese

Directions

1. Set your oven to 350 degrees before doing anything else.
2. Poke some holes into your pie crust and cook it in the oven for 12 mins. Then place everything to the side.
3. Now fry your bacon. And once it is crispy break it into pieces and place it to the side as well.
4. Get a bowl, combine: nutmeg, whisked eggs, mustard, and milk.
5. Get a 2nd bowl, combine: flour and bacon.
6. Add 3/4 of the coated bacon and cheese to the pie crust then top it with the egg mix.
7. Now add the rest of the bacon.
8. Cook everything in the oven for 60 mins. Then let the quiche sit for 15 mins.
9. Enjoy.

CHEDDAR
Mushroom Quiche (Vegetarian Approved)

 Prep Time: 30 mins

Total Time: 1 hr 40 mins

Servings per Recipe: 6

Calories	314 kcal
Fat	20.9 g
Carbohydrates	21.5g
Protein	11.2 g
Cholesterol	174 mg
Sodium	912 mg

Ingredients

1 tsp salt
1/2 C. diced zucchini
1 (9 in.) unbaked pastry shell
2 tbsps butter
1 1/2 C. diced onion
1 green bell pepper, diced
1 C. diced tomatoes
1/2 C. sliced fresh mushrooms
1 clove garlic, minced
1/4 tsp curry powder

1/2 tsp salt
1/4 tsp ground black pepper
1 pin. ground cinnamon
5 eggs
1/4 C. milk
1/4 C. grated Parmesan cheese
1/4 C. shredded Cheddar cheese

Directions

1. Coat your zucchini with 1 tsp of salt, in a bowl.
2. Let the veggies sit in the bowl, with the salt, for 12 mins. Then remove all the resulting liquids.
3. Cover a pie crust with foil and then set your oven to 450 degrees before doing anything else.
4. Cook the pie crust in the oven for 6 mins, with the foil, then take off the foil, and continue cooking the crust for 6 more mins.
5. Now set the oven to 350 degrees.
6. Stir fry your zucchini, onion, garlic, green pepper, green pepper, mushrooms, and tomatoes for 7 mins then add: cinnamon, curry powder, pepper, and half a tsp of salt.
7. Stir the contents and then pour everything into the pie crust.
8. Now get a bowl, combine: cheddar, whisked eggs, parmesan, and milk.
9. Pour this mix into the pie crust over the veggies.
10. Cook the quiche in the oven for 50 mins. Then let it cool for 10 mins. Enjoy.

Rustic Quiche

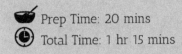 Prep Time: 20 mins

Total Time: 1 hr 15 mins

Servings per Recipe: 16
Calories	226 kcal
Fat	18.7 g
Carbohydrates	9.6g
Protein	5.4 g
Cholesterol	63 mg
Sodium	312 mg

Ingredients

1/2 lb beef sausage
3/4 lb sliced fresh mushrooms
1/4 C. butter
2 frozen pie crusts, thawed and ready to bake
1 C. heavy cream
2 eggs, beaten

1 tbsp all-purpose flour
1 tbsp melted butter
1 tbsp lemon juice
salt and pepper to taste
1/2 C. shredded Parmesan cheese

Directions

1. Set your oven to 400 degrees before doing anything else.
2. Cook your pie crust in the oven for 12 mins then set the oven's temp. to 350 degrees before doing anything else.
3. Remove the pie crust from the oven.
4. Stir fry your sausage until fully done and break the meat into pieces.
5. Then place the sausage on some paper towel to remove the excess oils.
6. Now begin to stir fry the mushrooms in butter and cook them for 7 mins.
7. Combine the mushrooms and the sausage in the pie dish.
8. Get a bowl, combine: pepper, cream, salt, eggs, lemon juice, flour, and butter.
9. Pour this mix into your pie crust and coat everything with the parmesan.
10. Place the quiche in the oven for 40 mins. Then let the contents cool for 7 mins.
11. Enjoy.

SEATTLE STYLE
Quiche

 Prep Time: 25 mins

🕐 Total Time: 1 hr

Servings per Recipe: 12

Calories	334 kcal
Fat	26.3 g
Carbohydrates	12.4g
Protein	12.4 g
Cholesterol	106 mg
Sodium	383 mg

Ingredients

1 lb fresh asparagus, trimmed and cut into 1/2 in. pieces
10 slices bacon
2 (8 in.) unbaked pie shells
1 egg white, lightly beaten
4 eggs
1 1/2 C. half-and-half cream

1/4 tsp ground nutmeg
salt and pepper to taste
2 C. shredded Swiss cheese

Directions

1. Set your oven to 400 degrees before doing anything else.
2. Steam your asparagus, over 2 inches of boiling water, in a saucepan, using a steamer insert.
3. Place a lid on the pot while the veggies steam and let them cook for 7 mins, then remove all the liquids.
4. Now begin to fry your bacon until it is fully done then break it into pieces.
5. Coat your pie crust with the egg whites and layer in your bacon and asparagus.
6. Get a bowl, combine: pepper, eggs, salt, cream, and nutmeg.
7. Pour this mix into your pie and cook everything in the oven for 37 mins.
8. Enjoy.

Broccoli, Lentils, and Tomato Quiche

🥣 Prep Time: 15 mins
🕐 Total Time: 1 hr 30 mins

Servings per Recipe: 8
Calories   165 kcal
Fat   9.1 g
Carbohydrates   12.4g
Protein   9.7 g
Cholesterol   103 mg
Sodium   392 mg

Ingredients

1 C. diced onion
2 tbsps olive oil
1/2 C. dried lentils
2 C. water
2 C. broccoli florets
1 C. diced fresh tomatoes
4 eggs, beaten

1 C. milk
1 tsp salt
ground black pepper to taste
2 tsps Italian seasoning
1/2 C. shredded Cheddar cheese (optional)

Directions

1. Set your oven to 375 degrees before doing anything else.
2. Coat your pie crust with olive oil and then layer the onions in it.
3. Cook the crust in the oven for 17 mins.
4. Get your water and lentils boiling.
5. Let the lentils cook for 22 mins. Then remove any excess liquids.
6. Layer the broccoli on over the lentils and place the lid on the pot and cook the mix for 7 mins.
7. Enter the tomatoes, broccoli, and lentils into the pie crust and stir the mix.
8. Add the cheese as well and stir again.
9. Get a bowl, combine: Italian seasoning, eggs, pepper, milk, and salt.
10. Enter this mix into your pie crust as well.
11. Cook everything in the oven for 50 mins then let the quiche cool for 10 mins.
12. Enjoy.

PEPPER
and Chicken
Quiche

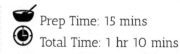

Prep Time: 15 mins
Total Time: 1 hr 10 mins

Servings per Recipe: 6

Calories	389 kcal
Fat	26.5 g
Carbohydrates	19.7g
Protein	17.6 g
Cholesterol	115 mg
Sodium	454 mg

Ingredients

1 (9 in.) frozen prepared pie crust,
thawed
1 tbsp olive oil
1/4 C. diced onion
1/4 C. diced green bell pepper
1 tbsp all-purpose flour
1 C. cooked, cubed chicken meat
1/4 tsp salt
1/4 tsp ground nutmeg
1/4 tsp ground black pepper

1/2 C. shredded sharp Cheddar cheese
1/2 C. shredded Swiss cheese
2 eggs, lightly beaten
3/4 C. milk
3/4 C. sour cream

Directions

1. Put your pie crust into a pie dish and then set your oven to 400 degrees before doing anything else.
2. Stir fry your bell peppers and onions in olive oil for 5 mins then add the flour and continue cooking the mix for 4 mins.
3. Now add the nutmeg, salt, pepper and chicken.
4. Mix the contents evenly.
5. Now put the chicken mix into your pie crust and place a covering of cheddar and Swiss cheese over the mix.
6. Get a bowl, combine: sour cream, milk, and whisked eggs.
7. Enter this mix into the pie crust as well.
8. Cook the pie in the oven for 22 mins then lower the temp to 350 degrees and cook the quiche for 32 more mins.
9. Enjoy.

Creamy
Romano and Swiss Quiche

Prep Time: 15 mins
Total Time: 1 hr

Servings per Recipe: 8

Calories	472 kcal
Fat	39.4 g
Carbohydrates	15.7g
Protein	14.9 g
Cholesterol	204 mg
Sodium	359 mg

Ingredients

2 tbsps butter
2 C. sliced leeks
1 (9 in.) frozen pie crust, thawed
1 C. shredded Swiss cheese
1/4 C. grated Romano cheese
1 tbsp all-purpose flour
4 eggs

1 3/4 C. heavy cream
1 tomato, thinly sliced
salt and pepper to taste

Directions

1. Set your oven to 450 degrees before doing anything else.
2. Stir fry your leeks in butter then layer them into the pie crust.
3. Get a bowl, combine: flour, Romano, and Swiss. Layer these cheeses over the veggies in the pie crust.
4. Get a 2nd bowl, combine: heavy cream and whisked eggs.
5. Now enter this mix into your pie crust and top everything with the pepper, salt, and tomato pieces.
6. Cook everything in the oven for 16 mins then set the oven's temp to 325 degrees and cook the quiche for 27 more mins.
7. Enjoy.

ARTISAN
Sun-Dried Pesto Quiche

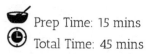

Prep Time: 15 mins
Total Time: 45 mins

Servings per Recipe: 8
Calories	222 kcal
Fat	16.1 g
Carbohydrates	13.1g
Protein	6.6 g
Cholesterol	81 mg
Sodium	235 mg

Ingredients

4 tbsps pesto
1 (9 in.) unbaked pie crust
4 tbsps crumbled goat cheese
3 eggs
1/2 C. half-and-half cream
1 tbsp all-purpose flour
8 oil-packed sun-dried tomatoes,

drained and cut into strips
salt and freshly ground black pepper to taste

Directions

1. Coat your pie dish with pesto and goat cheese then set your oven to 400 degrees before doing anything else.
2. Get a bowl, combine: pepper, flour, salt, cream, and whisked eggs.
3. Enter this into your pie crust and then layer the sun dried tomatoes over the mix.
4. Cook the quiche in the oven for 32 mins.
5. Enjoy.

A Quiche
from Maine

Prep Time: 45 mins

Total Time: 1 hr 20 mins

Servings per Recipe: 8	
Calories	154 kcal
Fat	9.3 g
Carbohydrates	6.7g
Protein	10.8 g
Cholesterol	99 mg
Sodium	289 mg

Ingredients

2 tbsps butter, divided
1/4 C. plain dried bread crumbs
2 C. 2% milk
8 oz. salmon fillets, skin removed
1/3 C. diced onion
1/2 bunch Swiss chard, diced
1/2 tsp salt

1/8 tsp ground black pepper
1/2 tsp dried marjoram
1/8 tsp ground nutmeg
3 eggs

Directions

1. Coat a pie dish with 1 tbsp of butter then set your oven to 350 degrees before doing anything else.
2. Now coat the pie dish with bread crumbs and shake off any excess.
3. Begin to simmer your salmon in milk, in a large pot with a lid.
4. Cook the salmon for 12 mins.
5. Now in a separate pan begin to stir fry your chards and onions in the rest of the butter.
6. Once all of the liquid has cooked out add: nutmeg, salt, marjoram, and pepper.
7. Remove everything from the pan and let the contents cool.
8. Enter the onion mix in to the pie dish and then flake your salmon into the mix as well.
9. Now get a bowl, combine: 1 C. of milk from the salmon and the eggs.
10. Pour this into the pie crust as well and cook everything in the oven for 40 mins.
11. Enjoy.

CHERRY TOMATOES
and Kale Quiche

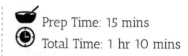

Prep Time: 15 mins
Total Time: 1 hr 10 mins

Servings per Recipe: 8
Calories   110 kcal
Fat   7 g
Carbohydrates   4.1g
Protein   8 g
Cholesterol   106 mg
Sodium   217 mg

Ingredients

1 C. diced kale
1 small leek, white and light green parts only, sliced
4 oz. halved cherry tomatoes
4 eggs
1 C. milk
4 oz. shredded Italian cheese blend

1 sprig fresh rosemary, finely diced
1 pin. sea salt
1/8 tsp ground black pepper
1 tbsp grated Parmesan cheese

Directions

1. Coat a pie plate with oil and then set your oven to 375 degrees before doing anything else.
2. Steam your kale over 2 inches of boiling water, in a large pot, using a steamer insert.
3. Place a lid on the pot and let the contents cook for 7 mins. Then place the kale into the pie plate.
4. Now combine the sliced tomatoes and leeks with the kale.
5. Get a bowl, combine: black pepper, milk, sea salt, cheese, and rosemary.
6. Enter this mix into the pie plate and stir the contents.
7. Cook everything in the oven for 35 mins.
8. Now place a topping of parmesan over the quiche and continue cooking it in the oven for 15 more mins.
9. Enjoy.

Nutty
Honey Quiche

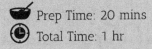 Prep Time: 20 mins
Total Time: 1 hr

Servings per Recipe: 8
Calories   586 kcal
Fat   47.4 g
Carbohydrates   34.1g
Protein   10.2 g
Cholesterol   175 mg
Sodium   468 mg

Ingredients

1/2 C. butter
1 C. sliced carrots
1 C. cashews
1/2 C. honey
3 eggs
1 1/2 C. heavy cream
1/2 tsp nutmeg

1/2 tsp salt
3/4 C. shredded Cheddar cheese
1 (9 in.) pie crust

Directions

1. Set your oven to 350 degrees before doing anything else.
2. Stir fry your cashews and carrots in melted butter until the carrots are soft.
3. Now add in your honey, stir the mix, and shut the heat.
4. Get a bowl, combine: salt, eggs, nutmeg, and heavy cream.
5. Layer your cheese into the pie dish and then place the cashew mix on top before pouring in the cream mix.
6. Cook everything in the oven for 38 mins.
7. Enjoy.

NUTTY
Tangy Chicken Quiche

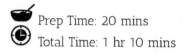
Prep Time: 20 mins
Total Time: 1 hr 10 mins

Servings per Recipe: 8
Calories	339 kcal
Fat	23 g
Carbohydrates	15.5g
Protein	18 g
Cholesterol	92 mg
Sodium	237 mg

Ingredients

1 C. diced, cooked chicken
1 C. shredded Swiss cheese
1/4 C. diced onion
1 tbsp all-purpose flour
1/2 C. diced pecans
1 (9 in.) unbaked deep-dish pastry shell
2 eggs, beaten

1 C. 2% milk
1/2 tsp brown mustard

Directions

1. Set your oven to 325 degrees before doing anything else.
2. Get a bowl, combine: 1/4 C. pecans, chicken, flour, cheese, and onions. Enter this into your pie.
3. Get a 2nd bowl, combine: mustard, the rest of the pecans, milk, and eggs. Layer this mix over the chicken mix in the pie crust and cook everything in the oven for 55 mins.
4. Enjoy.

Mexican Style
Quiche

Prep Time: 15 mins
Total Time: 1 hr 20 mins

Servings per Recipe: 8

Calories	520 kcal
Fat	36.4 g
Carbohydrates	23.1g
Protein	25.2 g
Cholesterol	208 mg
Sodium	1196 mg

Ingredients

1 (9 in.) unbaked deep-dish pie crust
10 oz. chorizo sausage
6 eggs
1/4 C. milk
1 (10 oz.) can diced tomatoes with green
chili peppers (such as RO*TEL(R)), drained

2 C. shredded Mexican cheese blend, divided
1 (15 oz.) can refried beans

Directions

1. Layer your pie crust into a pie dish and then set your oven to 400 degrees before doing anything else.
2. Stir fry your chorizo for 7 mins then break it into pieces.
3. Get a bowl, combine: milk and eggs. Then add in half of the cheese, the chili pepper, and the tomatoes. Stir everything together.
4. Layer your beans into the pie crust and evenly distribute them.
5. Now add in the chorizo and the egg mix. Top the quiche with the rest of the cheese.
6. Cook the quiche in the oven for 50 mins.
7. Enjoy.

ARTISAN STYLE
Spinach Quiche

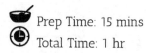

Prep Time: 15 mins
Total Time: 1 hr

Servings per Recipe: 6

Calories	274 kcal
Fat	17.1 g
Carbohydrates	19 g
Protein	11.4 g
Cholesterol	136 mg
Sodium	442 mg

Ingredients

1 (9 in.) unbaked pie crust
4 eggs
5 slices cooked bacon, crumbled
1/2 C. shredded mozzarella cheese
2 tbsps milk
2 tbsps all-purpose flour
2 cloves garlic, minced
1 tsp parsley

1/2 tsp thyme
1 C. spinach leaves, divided
1/2 C. canned artichoke hearts, drained and diced
2 roma (plum) tomatoes, sliced

Directions

1. Layer your pie crust into the pie plate then set your oven to 350 degrees before doing anything else.
2. Get a bowl, combine: thyme, eggs, parsley, bacon, garlic, mozzarella, flour, and milk.
3. Layer half of your spinach into the crust then add the artichokes on top.
4. Enter in the milk mix and then layer the tomato pieces on top of everything.
5. Cook the quiche in the oven for 50 mins.
6. Enjoy.

Really
Rustic Quiche

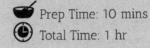 Prep Time: 10 mins

Total Time: 1 hr

Servings per Recipe: 6

Calories	462 kcal
Fat	31.5 g
Carbohydrates	20.2g
Protein	24.7 g
Cholesterol	183 mg
Sodium	993 mg

Ingredients

1 (3 oz.) can bacon bits
1/2 C. chopped onion
5 oz. shredded Swiss cheese
3 oz. grated Parmesan cheese
1 (9 inch) deep dish frozen pie crust

4 eggs, lightly beaten
1 C. half-and-half cream

Directions

1. Set your oven to 400 degrees before doing anything else.
2. Get a bowl, combine: all the cheeses, onions, and bacon.
3. Get a 2nd bowl, mix: half and half with the beaten eggs.
4. Combine both bowls and stir the contents.
5. Fill your crust with the mix and cook everything in the oven for 17 mins. Now set the heat of the oven to 350 and cook for 32 more mins.
6. Enjoy.

A QUICHE
of Squash and Mozzarella

Prep Time: 30 mins
Total Time: 1 hr 45 mins

Servings per Recipe: 6
Calories   145 kcal
Fat   4.5 g
Carbohydrates   12.9g
Protein   13 g
Cholesterol   37 mg
Sodium   279 mg

Ingredients

1/2 C. frozen chopped spinach , thawed, drained and squeezed dry
1/2 C. cooked, shredded spaghetti squash
1 beaten egg
3 egg whites
1 (12 fluid oz.) can evaporated skim milk

1 C. part-skim-milk mozzarella cheese
cooking spray
1/3 C. bread crumbs

Directions

1. Set your oven to 350 degrees before doing anything else.
2. Poke a few holes throughout your squash before cooking it in the microwave for 12 mins with high heat.
3. Now flip it over and cook for 9 more mins.
4. Once the squash is no longer hot, divide it into two pieces, take out the seeds, and then scrape out half a C. of the flesh into a bowl.
5. Add the following to the squash: spinach, egg, mozzarella, egg whites, and evaporated milk.
6. Coat a pie dish with some nonstick spray and then layer some bread crumbs at the bottom.
7. Now add the egg and squash mix to the dish.
8. Cook the dish for 45 mins in the oven then let it sit for 13 mins before serving.
9. Enjoy.

Swiss and Bacon Quiche

🥣 Prep Time: 30 mins
🕐 Total Time: 1 hr 5 mins

Servings per Recipe: 8
Calories	359 kcal
Fat	26.3 g
Carbohydrates	17g
Protein	13.6 g
Cholesterol	106 mg
Sodium	463 mg

Ingredients

1 recipe pastry for a 9 inch single crust pie
6 slices bacon
1 onion, sliced
3 eggs, beaten

1 1/2 C. milk
1/4 tsp salt
1 1/2 C. shredded Swiss cheese
1 tbsp all-purpose flour

Directions

1. Place some foil around a pastry shell and then set your oven to 450 degrees before doing anything else.
2. Cook the pastry for 9 mins in the oven then take off the foil and cook the contents for 4 more mins. Then place it on the counter.
3. Lower the heat of the oven to 325 degrees before continuing. Now stir fry your bacon, break it into pieces, and place it to the side.
4. Stir fry the onions in the drippings, until they are soft, and remove any excess oils.
5. Get a bowl, combine: eggs, salt, milk, onions, and bacon.
6. Get a 2nd bowl, combine: flour and cheese.
7. Combine both bowls and then fill your pastry shell with the mix.
8. Cook the quiche in the oven for 37 mins.
9. Serve when then pie has cooled off considerably. Enjoy.

NOVA SCOTIA
Quiche

Prep Time: 20 mins
Total Time: 1 hr

Servings per Recipe: 6

Calories	302 kcal
Fat	19.4 g
Carbohydrates	15.9 g
Protein	16.2 g
Cholesterol	141 mg
Sodium	898 mg

Ingredients

1 C. all-purpose baking mix
1/4 tsp salt
1/4 tsp ground black pepper
1/3 C. milk
3 slices turkey bacon, chopped
1 small onion, chopped
2 C. shredded Cheddar cheese
4 eggs

1 tsp salt
1/4 tsp hot pepper sauce
1 (12 fluid oz.) can evaporated milk, heated

Directions

1. Set your oven to 400 degrees F before doing anything else and grease a 9-inch pie dish.
2. Mix together the baking mix, salt and black pepper in a bowl.
3. Slowly, add the milk and mix till well combined and moistened.
4. Place the mixture onto a floured surface and knead till a dough forms.
5. With a rolling pin, roll the dough into a 12-inch round.
6. Transfer the dough into prepared pie pan and with your hands, press gently and then fold the edges.
7. Heat a large deep skillet on medium-high heat and cook bacon and onion till bacon is browned.
8. Drain the bacon and then crumble it.
9. Place the bacon and the onion mixture into the pie pan, followed by the cheese.
10. In a bowl, add the eggs, hot sauce and salt and beat till well combined and then mix in the hot evaporated milk.
11. Place the egg mixture over the cheese evenly and Cook everything in the oven for about 5 minutes.
12. Now, set the oven to 350 degrees F and cook for about 25 minutes or till set.

Quiche I
(Broccoli, Onions, and Mozzarella)

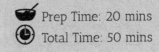 Prep Time: 20 mins

Total Time: 50 mins

Servings per Recipe: 6

Calories	371 kcal
Fat	24.9 g
Carbohydrates	21.5g
Protein	16.1 g
Cholesterol	162 mg
Sodium	885 mg

Ingredients

2 tbsps butter
1 onion, minced
1 tsp minced garlic
2 C. chopped fresh broccoli
1 (9 inch) unbaked pie crust
1 1/2 C. shredded mozzarella cheese
4 eggs, well beaten

1 1/2 C. milk
1 tsp salt
1/2 tsp black pepper
1 tbsp butter, melted

Directions

1. Set your oven to 350 degrees before doing anything else.
2. Get a bowl, mix: milk and eggs.
3. Stir fry your broccoli, onions, and garlic in melted butter until everything is tender.
4. Add the veggies into the pie and top with cheese.
5. Add the milk mixture, melted butter, pepper and salt.
6. Cook the quiche in the oven for 40 mins.
7. Enjoy.

A QUICHE
of Broccoli

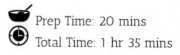 Prep Time: 20 mins
Total Time: 1 hr 35 mins

Servings per Recipe: 4
Calories	320 kcal
Fat	14.7 g
Carbohydrates	33.5g
Protein	14.8 g
Cholesterol	140 mg
Sodium	575 mg

Ingredients

2 large potatoes, peeled
2 C. chopped fresh broccoli
1/4 C. milk
1/4 tsp salt
1 tbsp olive oil
1/2 onion, chopped
1 C. shredded Cheddar cheese
3 eggs

1 C. milk
1/2 tsp salt
1/2 tsp ground black pepper
1/4 tsp ground nutmeg

Directions

1. Set your oven to 350 degrees before doing anything else.
2. Boil your potatoes in water and salt for 17 mins then remove all the liquids.
3. At the same time steam your broccoli, using a steamer insert, in a pot of 2 inches of boiling water.
4. Steam the veggies for 5 mins then remove all the liquids.
5. Begin to mash your potatoes and then add in some salt and continue mashing. Then combine in the milk and mash everything again.
6. Coat a pie dish with olive oil then layer your potatoes at the bottom of the dish.
7. Add some more olive oil then cook the crust in the oven for 32 mins.
8. Then layer your cheese, onions, and broccoli in the pie dish.
9. Get a bowl, combine: the nutmeg, eggs, pepper, milk, and salt.
10. Pour this mix into the pie dish and cook everything in the oven for 35 mins.
11. Let the quiche cool for 15 mins.
12. Enjoy.

Southern French
Quiche

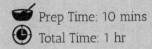 Prep Time: 10 mins
Total Time: 1 hr

Servings per Recipe: 6
Calories   365 kcal
Fat   26.8 g
Carbohydrates   20.7g
Protein   11.2 g
Cholesterol   57 mg
Sodium   300 mg

Ingredients

1 (9 inch) refrigerated pie crust
2 tsps butter
3 leeks, diced
1 pinch salt and black pepper to taste

1 C. light cream
1 1/4 C. shredded Gruyere cheese

Directions

1. Set your oven to 375 degrees before doing anything else.
2. Sauté your leeks in butter for 12 mins then add some pepper and salt.
3. Set the heat to low and add in the cheese and cream.
4. Stir the mix to get it smooth then fill your pie with the mixture.
5. Cook the pie in the oven for 32 mins then let it rest on a countertop for 15 mins before serving.
6. Enjoy.

SOUTHWEST
Quiches

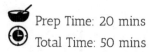 Prep Time: 20 mins
Total Time: 50 mins

Servings per Recipe: 12
Calories	151.4
Fat	8.2g
Cholesterol	48.3mg
Sodium	556.7mg
Carbohydrates	8.7g
Protein	10.5g

Ingredients

1 lb lean ground beef
1/3 C. chopped onion
1/3 C. sliced black olives
1 cans tomato sauce
1/4 C. water
1 packages taco seasoning mix
2 tbsp hot sauce
1 egg, beaten

4 flour tortillas
1/3 C. sour cream
1/2 C. shredded cheddar cheese

Directions

1. Before you do anything, preheat the oven to 350 F. Grease a muffin pan.
2. Place a large pan over medium heat. Brown in it the onion with beef for 8 min. Discard the fat.
3. Mix in the olives, tomato sauce, 1/4 C. water, taco seasoning, hot sauce and egg. Turn off the heat.
4. Use 3 inches cookie cutter circle to cut each tortilla into 3 rounds. Place the tortilla circles in the greased muffin C.
5. Spoon the beef mixture over the tortilla C. Top them with sour cream and cheese. Cook them for 26 min in the oven.
6. Serve your taco muffins with your favorite toppings.
7. Enjoy.

Roasted Veggies Quiche

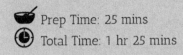 Prep Time: 25 mins

Total Time: 1 hr 25 mins

Servings per Recipe: 6	
Calories	481.4
Fat	34.6g
Cholesterol	107.9mg
Sodium	373.4mg
Carbohydrates	30.7g
Protein	12.6g

Ingredients

12 oz frozen shortcrust pastry, thawed
1 red onion, quatered
1 red bell pepper, de-seeded and chopped
1 yellow bell pepper, de-seeded and chopped
1 zucchini, sliced thickly
1 tbsp olive oil

2 large eggs
4 1/2 fluid oz cream
4 oz gruyere or 4 oz mature cheddar cheese, grated

Directions

1. Before you do anything set the oven to 425 F. Grease a flan or pie pan.
2. Roll the pastry on a working surface and place it in the pan. Cover it with a piece of a parchment paper and fill it with beans. Cook it in it the oven for 12 min.
3. Remove the parchment paper with beans and cook them for 6 min. Place the quiche shell aside.
4. Toss all the veggies with oil on a baking sheet. Cook them for 38 min. Place the veggies aside to lose heat completely.
5. Lower the oven heat to 350 F.
6. Get a large bowl: Mix in it the milk with eggs. Fold in the cheese with a pinch of salt and pepper.
7. Fill the quiche shell with the roasted veggies and pour the eggs mix all over them. Cook the quiche for 36 min. Serve it warm.
8. Enjoy.

ALGERIAN
Quiche

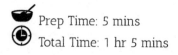 Prep Time: 5 mins

Total Time: 1 hr 5 mins

Servings per Recipe: 10

Calories	174.8
Fat	12.6g
Cholesterol	18.6mg
Sodium	719.3mg
Carbohydrates	10.7g
Protein	4.7g

Ingredients

2 C. chickpea flour
4 C. water
1/2 C. oil
1 tbsp. salt
1/4 tsp. black pepper

1 egg, beaten
ground cumin, for sprinkling
harissa

Directions

1. Before you do anything, preheat the oven to 375 F.
2. Place the flour with water, oil, salt and pepper in a blender.
3. Pulse them several times until they become smooth. Pour it into a mixing bowl.
4. Add to it the beaten egg and mix them well. Pour the mixture into a greased pie pan.
5. Bake it for 60 min until it becomes golden brown.
6. Allow the pie to cool down for few minutes then top it with the harissa.
7. Serve it right away.
8. Enjoy.

Wonda's Award Winning Quiche

Prep Time: 30 mins
Total Time: 1 hr 10 mins

Servings per Recipe: 8
Calories	377.3
Fat	25.0g
Cholesterol	190.9mg
Sodium	427.1mg
Carbohydrates	26.4g
Protein	13.2g

Ingredients

1 tbsp butter
1/2 C. vegetable stock
2 leeks, washed and chopped
1 large onion, diced
30 Brussels sprouts, peeled and quartered
2 garlic cloves, minced
1 spring onion, sliced
1 tbsp herbs de Provence
5 oz. Philadelphia Cream Cheese

1 C. cheese, grated
1/2 C. cream
6 eggs, beaten
salt
pepper
1 (30 cm) unbaked pie shells

Directions

1. Place a large skillet over medium heat.
2. Combine in it the onion with butter, stock, leeks, brussels sprouts, garlic, spring onion, and herbs de Provence.
3. Cook them for 8 min while stirring them often. Turn off the heat and let them cool down for a while.
4. Stir in the cream cheese with cheese, cream, eggs, a pinch of salt and pepper.
5. Spoon the mixture into the pie shell. Bake it for 42 min.
6. Serve your pie warm.
7. Enjoy.

LUCIA'S
Quiche Caprese

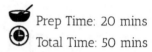

Prep Time: 20 mins
Total Time: 50 mins

Servings per Recipe: 6
Calories   110.7
Fat   8.0g
Cholesterol   155.9mg
Sodium   64.5mg
Carbohydrates   4.1g
Protein   5.6g

Ingredients

4 eggs
1 C. half-and-half
1 tbsp chopped basil
1 tsp ground pepper
1/3 lb. chopped prosciutto, or turkey bacon

1/2 C. chopped onion, sautéed
1/2 C. diced tomato, seeds removed
1 C. shredded Italian cheese blend

Directions

1. Set your oven to 375 degrees F before doing anything else and grease a 9-inch pie dish.
2. In a bowl, add the half-and-half and eggs and beat until combined nicely.
3. Add the remaining ingredients and gently, stir to combine.
4. Transfer the egg mixture into the prepared pie dish evenly.
5. Cook in the oven for about 35 minutes.
6. Remove from the oven and keep aside for about 10-12 minutes before slicing.
7. Cut into desired sized slices and enjoy.

Monterey
Mushroom Quiche

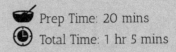 Prep Time: 20 mins
Total Time: 1 hr 5 mins

Servings per Recipe: 4

Calories	798.8
Fat	59.3g
Cholesterol	251.2mg
Sodium	1134.5mg
Carbohydrates	32.3g
Protein	35.6g

Ingredients

2 tbsp vegetable oil
1 C. chopped onion
1 tsp dried thyme, chopped
1 tsp dried basil, chopped
2 C. chopped broccoli, crowns & stems
2 C. sliced mushrooms
5 cloves garlic, chopped
salt
3 eggs, beaten

3/4 C. feta cheese
2 1/2 C. cheddar cheese, grated
1/2 C. Monterey jack cheese, grated
salt & pepper
1 unbaked pie crust

Directions

1. Before you do anything, preheat the oven to 375 F.
2. Place a pan over medium heat and heat the oil.
3. Cook in it the onions, thyme, basil, garlic and broccoli for 4 min.
4. Stir in the mushroom with a pinch of salt. Cook them for 4 min. Discard the excess liquid.
5. Place the pie crust in a lined up pie pan. Pour the mixture into it.
6. Get a mixing bowl: Whisk in it the eggs with cheeses, a pinch of salt and pepper.
7. Pour it all over the broccoli layer. Place the pan in the oven and let it cook for 46 min.
8. Allow the quiche to sit for 6 min. Serve it warm.
9. Enjoy.

MARIE'S
Quiche

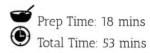

Prep Time: 18 mins
Total Time: 53 mins

Servings per Recipe: 6
Calories   117.9
Fat   2.0g
Cholesterol   5.3mg
Sodium   257.3mg
Carbohydrates   13.0g
Protein   12.5g

Ingredients

2 C. sliced mushrooms
1 onion, diced medium
10 oz. chopped spinach, thawed and
squeezed dry
1/4 C. plain breadcrumbs
2 C. skim milk

8 egg whites
1/4 C. parmesan cheese
1 tsp garlic powder
1 tsp Italian seasoning
1/2 tsp cracked black pepper

Directions

1. Before you do anything, preheat the oven to 350 F.
2. Place a pan over medium heat. Heat in it 2 tbsp of water. Cook in the onion for 3 min.
3. Stir in the spinach and cook them for 5 min. Stir in the breadcrumbs with a pinch of salt and pepper.
4. Spoon the mixture into a greased baking pan. Spread it in an even layer.
5. Get a mixing bowl: Toss in it all the remaining ingredients. Pour it over the spinach layer.
6. Place everything in the oven. Let it cook for 36 to 46 min.
7. Allow the quiche to rest for 6 min. Serve it with some hot sauce.
8. Enjoy.

Saint Claude
Quiche

Prep Time: 20 mins
Total Time: 50 mins

Servings per Recipe: 4
Calories	329.9
Fat	12.1g
Cholesterol	73.9mg
Sodium	949.7mg
Carbohydrates	34.6g
Protein	19.3g

Ingredients

2 C. cooked white rice
1 tsp garlic powder
1 tsp onion powder
1/2 tsp salt
1 large egg, lightly beaten
cooking spray
1 oz. cheddar cheese, shredded
1/2 C. onion, diced
1/2 C. celery, diced
1/2 C. red bell pepper, diced
1 tsp garlic, minced

3 oz. Andouille sausages
3/4 C. egg substitute
2 large egg whites, lightly beaten
1/4 C. plain yogurt
1/4 tsp salt
1/4 tsp hot pepper sauce
1 oz. cheddar cheese

Directions

1. Before you do anything, preheat the oven to 375 F.
2. Get a large mixing bowl: Mix in it the white rice with garlic powder, onion powder, salt and beaten egg.
3. Pour the mix into a greased baking glass dish. Top it with 1/4 C. of cheese.
4. Place a large pan over medium heat. Heat a splash of oil in it. Cook in it the onion with celery, bell pepper, garlic and sausage. Cook them for 6 min.
5. Spread the mix over the rice layer.
6. Get a mixing bowl: Whisk in it the egg substitute with egg whites, yogurt, salt and hot pepper sauce. Spread the mix over the veggies layer.
7. Sprinkle the remaining cheese on top. Place the casserole in the oven and let it cook for 35 min. serve it warm.
8. Enjoy.

LOS ANGELES
Monterey Quiche

Prep Time: 20 mins
Total Time: 55 mins

Servings per Recipe: 6
Calories	332.1
Fat	24.9g
Cholesterol	145.8mg
Sodium	340.2mg
Carbohydrates	14.7g
Protein	12.5g

Ingredients

1 ready-made pie crust
1 tbsp cooking oil
1/4 C. onion, chopped
1 clove garlic, crushed
1/2 C. red bell pepper , chopped
1/2 C. green bell pepper, chopped

1 1/2 C. Monterey jack cheese
3 large eggs
1 C. half-and-half milk
1/2 tsp dried basil

Directions

1. Set your oven to 425 degrees F before doing anything else.
2. Place a pie crust into 9-inch pie plate and gently, press to fit.
3. Cook in the oven for about 8 minutes.
4. For the filling: in a 10-inch skillet, heat oil and sauté the onion and garlic for about 1 minute.
5. Add the peppers and cook for about 2-3 minutes.
6. Place the peppers mixture over cooked pie crust and sprinkle with cheese.
7. In a small bowl, add half-and-half, eggs and basil and beat until well combined.
8. Carefully pour egg mixture over pepper mixture evenly.
9. Cook in the oven for about 15 minutes.
10. Now, set the oven to 350 degrees F and cook the quiche for about 20 minutes.

Brown Ham
Quiche

🥄 Prep Time: 20 mins
🕐 Total Time: 1 hr 20 mins

Servings per Recipe: 6
Calories	419.5
Fat	28.5g
Cholesterol	153.3mg
Sodium	536.1mg
Carbohydrates	20.1g
Protein	21.1g

Ingredients

3 C. frozen shredded hash browns, thawed and drained well
1/3 C. butter, melted
1 1/2 C. cooked turkey ham, diced into very small pieces
1 1/2 C. shredded sharp cheddar cheese

2 eggs
1/2 C. milk
1/2 tsp salt
1/4 tsp fresh ground pepper

Directions

1. Before you do anything, preheat the oven to 425 F. Coat a baking pie pan with some butter.
2. Pat the hash browns dry then press it to the bottom of the baking pan. Pour the melted butter all over it to make the crust.
3. Place the crust pan in the oven and let it cook for 26 min.
4. Get a large mixing bowl: Mix in it the cheese with ham.
5. Get another mixing bowl: Whisk in it the eggs, milk, salt and pepper.
6. Spread the ham and cheese over the hash brown crust then top it with the eggs mix. Place the pan in the oven and let it cook for 28 to 32 min.
7. Allow the quiche to sit for 12 min then serve it.
8. Enjoy.

PUMPKIN
Quiche

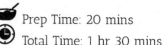 Prep Time: 20 mins

Total Time: 1 hr 30 mins

Servings per Recipe: 8

Calories	274
Fat	11.2g
Cholesterol	106mg
Sodium	440mg
Carbohydrates	39.5g
Protein	8.4g

Ingredients

For Pumpkin Layer:
1 small pumpkin, peeled, seeded and chopped
2 carrots, peeled and chopped
1 large sweet potato, peeled and chopped
2 eggs, beaten
2 tbsp olive oil
2 tbsp butter, melted
3 tbsp brown sugar
½ tsp curry powder
½ tsp ground cinnamon
¼ tsp ground cumin

Pinch of ground nutmeg
½ tsp salt
For Spinach Layer:
1 (16 oz.) package frozen chopped spinach, thawed and drained
½ C. half-and-half cream
2 eggs
½ tsp salt
¼ tsp freshly ground black pepper
2 tbsp bread crumbs

Directions

1. For pumpkin layer in a large pan of water, add pumpkin, carrots and sweet potato and bring to a boil on high heat.
2. Reduce the heat to low. Cook for about 40 minutes or till vegetables become very tender. Drain well.
3. Set your oven to 350 degrees F. Grease a 12-inch pie dish.
4. In a large food processor, add cooked vegetables and remaining all ingredients till smooth and well combined.
5. Transfer the vegetable mixture in a bowl.
6. Wirth paper towel, wipe out the food processor.
7. For spinach layer in food processor, add all ingredients except bread crumbs and pulse till smooth.
8. Stir in bread crumbs.

9. Transfer the spinach mixture in prepared pie dish evenly. With the back of spatula, flatten the surface.
10. Now, place the vegetable mixture over spinach mixture evenly.
11. With a spoon, gently, mix the both mixture to make a marbled pattern.
12. Bake for about 30 minutes or till top becomes golden brown.

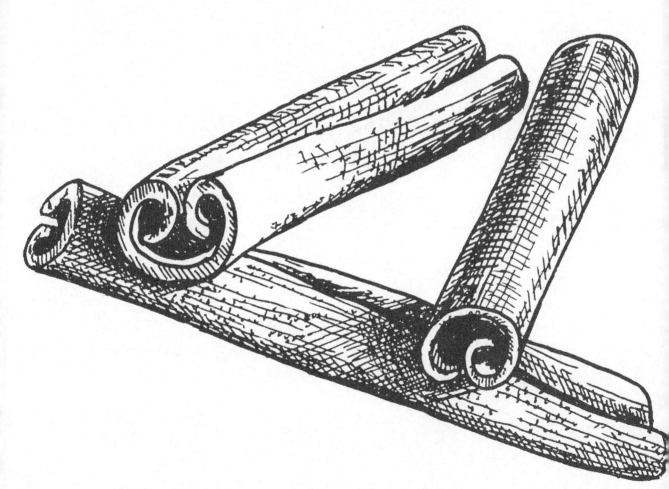

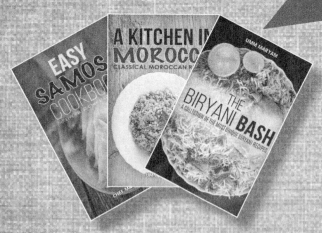

Printed in Great Britain
by Amazon

43997245R00044